WONDERS OF
THE WORLD

Wonders of the World

Mount Kilimanjaro

The World's Tallest Free-standing Mountain

Galadriel Watson

www.av2books.com

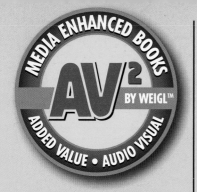

AV² provides enriched content that supplements and complements this book Weigl's AV² books strive to create inspired learning and engage young minds in a total learning experience.

Your AV² Media Enhanced books come alive with...

Audio
Listen to sections of the book read aloud.

Key Words
Study vocabulary, and complete a matching word activity.

Video
Watch informative video clips.

Quizzes
Test your knowledge.

Embedded Weblinks
Gain additional information for research.

Slide Show
View images and captions, and prepare a presentation.

Try This!
Complete activities and hands-on experiments.

... and much, much more!

Go to **www.av2books.com,** and enter this book's unique code.

BOOK CODE

J322820

AV² by Weigl brings you media enhanced books that support active learning.

Published by AV² by Weigl
350 5th Avenue, 59th Floor
New York, NY 10118
Website: www.av2books.com   www.weigl.com

Library of Congress Cataloging-in-Publication Data

Watson, Galadriel Findlay.
  Mount Kilimanjaro / Galadriel Watson.
     p. cm. -- (Wonders of the world)
  Includes index.
  ISBN 978-1-62127-476-6 (hardcover : alk. paper) -- ISBN 978-1-62127-482-7 (softcover : alk. paper)
  1. Kilimanjaro, Mount (Tanzania)--Juvenile literature. I. Title.
  DK449.K4W38 2013
  916.7826--dc23

                              2012040448

Printed in the United States of America in North Mankato, Minnesota
1 2 3 4 5 6 7 8 9   17 16 15 14 13 12

122012
WEP301112

Editor Heather Kissock
Design Mandy Christiansen

Every reasonable effort has been made to trace ownership and to obtain permission to reprint copyright material. The publishers would be pleased to have any errors or omissions brought to their attention so that they may be corrected in subsequent printings.

Photo Credits
Weigl acknowledges Getty Images as its primary photo supplier for this title.

Contents

The Pride of Tanzania

Rising high above the plains of Tanzania, Mount Kilimanjaro is the tallest mountain in Africa. Mount Kilimanjaro stands alone. It is not part of a mountain chain and is not connected to any other mountain. It is the tallest free-standing mountain in the world.

Mount Kilimanjaro ranks as one of the biggest volcanoes on Earth, although it is actually made up of three volcanoes. The tallest of the three is a cone-shaped volcano named Kibo. Its highest peak rises 19,340 feet (5,895 meters) above sea level. Mawenzi is shorter and has a jagged peak. Shira collapsed long ago and has eroded, or worn away, so much that its once jagged peak has become a flat **plateau.**

Mount Kilimanjaro attracts visitors from around the world. Approximately 25,000 people attempt to climb Kilimanjaro every year.

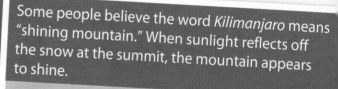

Some people believe the word *Kilimanjaro* means "shining mountain." When sunlight reflects off the snow at the summit, the mountain appears to shine.

Mount Kilimanjaro Facts

- Mawenzi, Shira, and Kibo are all considered to be extinct. This means that they are no longer active volcanoes.
- Mount Kilimanjaro can be seen from a distance of more than 120 miles (190 kilometers).

- The three volcanoes that make up Mount Kilimanjaro cover an area about 40 miles (60 km) long and 50 miles (80 km) wide.
- The highest point on Mount Kilimanjaro is Uhuru Peak. It is located on Kibo.

Map of Mount Kilimanjaro

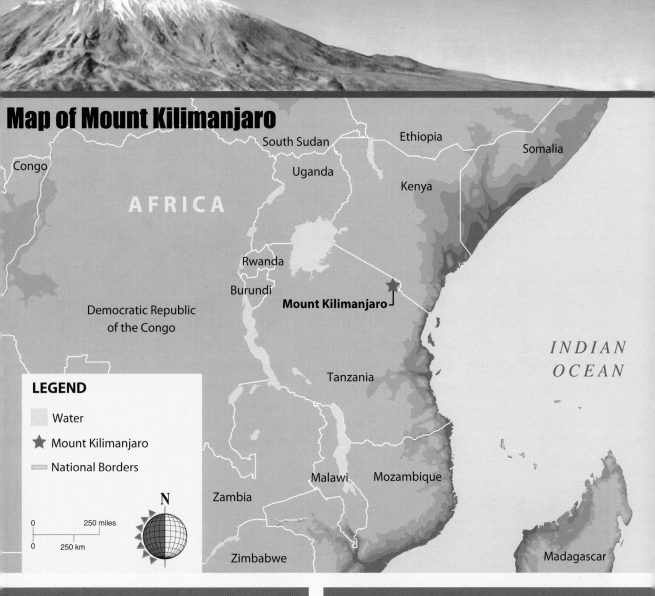

Congo

South Sudan

Ethiopia

Somalia

Uganda

AFRICA

Kenya

Rwanda

Burundi

Mount Kilimanjaro

Democratic Republic
of the Congo

INDIAN
OCEAN

Tanzania

LEGEND

Water

★ Mount Kilimanjaro

National Borders

N

0   250 miles

0   250 km

Zambia

Malawi

Mozambique

Zimbabwe

Madagascar

Elephants can be found in the forests on the northern slopes and surrounding areas of Mount Kilimanjaro.

The range of temperatures on Mount Kilimanjaro provides for a wide variety of plant life, including mosses, lichens, and flowers.

Where in the World?

Tanzania is the largest country in eastern Africa. It became a country in 1964, when the countries of Tanganyika and Zanzibar merged. Tanzania is home to more than 46 million people. It is one of the poorest countries in Africa and the world.

Mount Kilimanjaro sits in the northeastern part of Tanzania, bordering on Kenya. The mountain is about 170 miles (270 km) west of the Indian Ocean and 220 miles (350 km) south of the **equator**. The Great Rift Valley lies about 100 miles (160 km) west of Mount Kilimanjaro. The forces that created this valley played a key role in the mountain's formation.

Poaching has caused the black rhinoceros population to decline by 90 percent since 1960. Black rhinos are now extinct in the area around Kilimanjaro.

Rift valleys form where the Earth's crust spreads apart. The rift responsible for the creation of Mount Kilimanjaro has been forming for approximately 30 million years.

Puzzler

Mount Kilimanjaro is the highest mountain on the continent of Africa. The highest mountains for all of the continents, sometimes called the Seven Summits, are listed below. Using an atlas or the internet, match the mountain to the correct continent.

1. North America
2. South America
3. Europe
4. Antarctica
5. Asia
6. Australia
7. Africa

A. Mount Elbrus
B. Vinson Massif
C. Mount Kilimanjaro
D. Mount Kosciuszko
E. Mount Aconcagua
F. Mount McKinley/Denali
G. Mount Everest

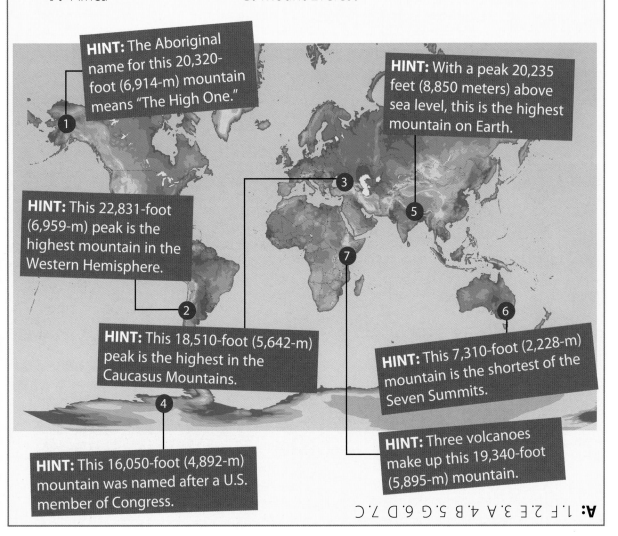

HINT: The Aboriginal name for this 20,320-foot (6,914-m) mountain means "The High One."

HINT: With a peak 20,235 feet (8,850 meters) above sea level, this is the highest mountain on Earth.

HINT: This 22,831-foot (6,959-m) peak is the highest mountain in the Western Hemisphere.

HINT: This 18,510-foot (5,642-m) peak is the highest in the Caucasus Mountains.

HINT: This 7,310-foot (2,228-m) mountain is the shortest of the Seven Summits.

HINT: This 16,050-foot (4,892-m) mountain was named after a U.S. member of Congress.

HINT: Three volcanoes make up this 19,340-foot (5,895-m) mountain.

A: 1.F 2.E 3.A 4.B 5.G 6.D 7.C

A Trip Back in Time

Mount Kilimanjaro began forming more than 750,000 years ago. The mountain was created as a result of volcanic activity that started deep underground and broke through to the surface.

The mountain-building process did not happen overnight. It took more than 250,000 years for Mount Kilimanjaro to form. Shira was the first volcano to emerge. Mawenzi was next. Finally, about 460,000 years ago, Kibo came to be. The **lava** that flowed from Kibo attached all three volcanoes together, making the mountain that stands today.

Over time, the shape of the mountain became more defined. During the course of several **ice ages**, huge sheets of ice called glaciers cut through the rock, carving it into smooth valleys and sharp ridges.

Mount Kilimanjaro is a stratovolcano, meaning it is cone-shaped and gets gradually steeper toward the top. Stratovolcanoes are formed by many layers of lava, ash, and other volcanic materials building up over time.

How a Volcano Forms

Most volcanoes, including Shira, Kibo, and Mawenzi, occur between two tectonic plates. Some volcanoes, such as the Hawai'ian Islands, occur in the middle of one plate.

A thin layer of rock, called the crust, covers Earth. Beneath the crust lies a layer of melted rock called magma. The crust is broken into several pieces, called tectonic plates. These plates float around on the layer of magma. Sometimes, they bump into each other or pull apart. This movement can wear away parts of the crust, creating cracks and thin spots. Magma can burst through these weak spots. When this happens, land is pushed up, and the magma, called lava when it is above ground, spills out. This creates a volcano.

Mount Kilimanjaro was formed because of activity in the nearby Great Rift Valley, a place where two plates are pulling apart. Lava burst through the **fault** that makes up the valley. The force of the lava pushed part of Earth's crust upwards, creating the first of Kilimanjaro's three volcanoes, Shira. Similar activity later created the other two volcanoes.

Kilimanjaro's Plants

D ue to its massive size, Mount Kilimanjaro is home to five **vegetation** zones. Each zone occurs at a different **altitude** and has unique features.

Above 16,400 feet (5,000 m), there is very little life. The fifth zone, or summit area, is home only to rocks, snow, and a few lichens.

Few plants can stand the cold, dry conditions at 13,120 to 16,400 feet (4,000 to 5,000 m). This fourth zone is a hot, dry desert during the day, but the ground freezes at night. Only everlastings, mosses, **lichens**, and three types of grasses are able to survive here.

The third zone occurs at 9,200 to 13,120 feet (2,800 to 4,000 m). Vegetation made up of **heath**, grasses, giant groundsels and lobelias, and other wildflowers cover the slopes in this zone.

At 5,900 to 9,200 feet (1,800 to 2,800 m), the second zone is a humid rain forest. Here, there is an abundance of plant life. Moss drapes the huge fig, juniper, date palm, and olive trees.

The first zone is found on the lower slopes of Kilimanjaro, between 2,300 and 5,900 feet (700 and 1,800 m). At one time, the land in this zone was covered with forest and scrub. Today, the rich soils make it perfect for farming. Wildflowers are common in this zone.

Giant Plants

To survive the cold, dry climate at the top of a mountain, most plants remain small. By being small, they need less water and sunlight than larger plants do. However, on Mount Kilimanjaro, some plants grow to be very large, even as the altitude increases.

On the mountain, lobelias and groundsels can grow to be as tall as a giraffe. The scorching temperatures of an African day help these plants survive at higher altitudes. However, at night, temperatures are freezing. To keep warm, both types of plants absorb heat from the Sun and store it in a unique way.

The groundsel does not shed dead leaves. Instead, the leaves remain on the plant's trunk as a form of **insulation**. The lobelia has tough outer leaves that close around the inner leaves and buds. They release a slimy substance that helps keep the plant from freezing.

Lobelia deckenii is a type of giant lobelia that grows in the mountains of east Africa.

Life on Mount Kilimanjaro

Mount Kilimanjaro is home to many animals, including 140 types of mammals. Each vegetation zone has unique features that support different creatures. While some zones have a large variety of wildlife, others are inhabited by only the smallest life forms.

In the lush rain forest of the second zone, the trees are alive with monkeys and birds. Large animals, including elephants, lions, leopards, and giraffes, travel through the jungle growth. African hunting dogs and birds of prey, such as buzzards, eagles, and bearded vultures, live here as well.

The extreme altitude keeps many animals from living higher up the mountain. Lions, wild dogs, and elands have been found living in the third zone. Even fewer animals dwell in the fourth zone. These include birds, rodents, and insects. Animals are unable to survive the harsh climates of the fifth zone.

The blue monkey is one of three primate species found in the montane forests of Mount Kilimanjaro. Its face is usually dark, but rarely is it actually blue in color.

Elands

Elands are the largest and slowest antelopes in the world. Their maximum running speed is only about 25 miles (40 km) per hour.

Elands are some of the many mammals that live on Mount Kilimanjaro. These large animals look similar to cows and can grow to be about 6.6 feet (2 m) high at the shoulders. They weigh between 600 and 2,200 pounds (270 and 1,000 kilograms).

Male and female elands have long, twisting horns that grow from the top of their head. As they age, eland fur turns from tan to gray to black.

In addition to Kilimanjaro, elands can be found living in the grasslands of central and southern Africa. Here, they graze on plant matter, such as twigs, branches, grasses, and leaves.

Early Explorers

Johannes Rebmann, a German **missionary**, arrived in East Africa in 1846. Rebmann traveled the countryside to teach Africans about **Christianity**. On May 11, 1848, he became the first European to see Mount Kilimanjaro.

Rebmann reported his find back to Europe. However, few people believed he had found a snow-covered mountain in Africa, so close to the equator. Support for Rebmann's claims came 12 years later. German explorer Baron Karl Klaus von der Decken and British geologist Richard Thornton surveyed the mountain. They were the first Europeans to see Mount Kilimanjaro since Rebmann had visited the site.

Decken and Thornton attempted to climb the mountain. However, bad weather stopped them from climbing very high. In 1862, when Decken and explorer Otto Kersten made another attempt to climb Mount Kilimanjaro, poor weather stopped their team at about 14,000 feet (4,267 m). Twenty-seven years passed before Hans Meyer and Ludwig Purtscheller became the first Europeans to reach the top of the mountain.

Ludwig Purtscheller was a mountain climber from Austria. He was 40 years old when he and Hans Meyer summited Mount Kilimanjaro.

Biography

Hans Meyer (1858–1929)

As a child, Hans Meyer enjoyed learning about geography. His family published books, and Meyer often read about faraway places. At age 23, he left home and traveled around the world for two years. Meyer then worked as a professor of geography at Germany's Leipzig University.

In 1887, Meyer made his first attempt to climb Mount Kilimanjaro. He was poorly equipped and had to turn back. Meyer tried again the next year, but a war in the area kept him from completing the trek. The following year, Meyer returned with Austrian climber Ludwig Purtscheller. On October 6, 1889, Meyer and Purtscheller became the first Europeans to reach the highest peak, Kibo's summit. Meyer planted a German flag on the summit.

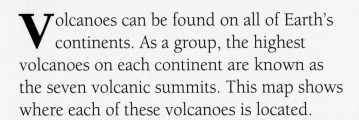

The Big Picture

Volcanoes can be found on all of Earth's continents. As a group, the highest volcanoes on each continent are known as the seven volcanic summits. This map shows where each of these volcanoes is located.

Pico de Orizaba
Mexico
18,491 feet (5,636 m)

NORTH AMERICA

ATLA
OC

Ojos del Salado
Argentina and Chile
22,572 feet (6,880 m)

EQUATOR

PACIFIC
OCEAN

SOUTH
AMERICA

Mount Sidley
Antarctica
14,058 feet (4,285 m)

SOUTHE
OCEAN

ANTARCTICA

ARCTIC OCEAN

ASIA

EUROPE

Damavand
Iran
18,406 feet (5,610 m)

Mount Giluwe
Papua New Guinea
14,331 feet (4,368 m)

PACIFIC
OCEAN

AFRICA

EQUATOR

Mount Elbrus
Russia
18,510 feet (5,642 m)

AUSTRALIA

Mount Kilimanjaro
Tanzania
19,340 feet (5,895 m)

SOUTHERN
OCEAN

LEGEND

☐ Ocean

🪝 River

Scale at Equator

0	1,000	2,000	3,000 miles
0	1,000	2,000	3,000 km

N

Living on Kilimanjaro

Archaeologists have found stone bowls at the base of Mount Kilimanjaro. These show that people have lived near the mountain for at least 3,000 years. Today, the area is inhabited mostly by a group of people called the Chagga.

The Chagga have lived in the area around Mount Kilimanjaro for about 400 years. One of Tanzania's largest cultural groups, the Chagga reside on the lower levels of the mountain. They use the land for farming, taking advantage of the rich soils and plentiful water that runs from the mountain's glaciers. Important crops include coffee and bananas, as well as barley, wheat, and sugar. The Chagga raise cattle, and some people collect honey.

Some Chagga still practice the traditional ways of their ancestors. Many groups have adopted European beliefs and ways of life. They attend university and work in fields such as medicine and law. In most cases, the guides and porters that travel with tourists as they climb Kilimanjaro are Chagga.

In Chagga society, women are responsible for cooking, gathering firewood, and cleaning the home.

Language Essentials

Most of the people in Tanzania speak a language called Swahili. The Chagga people that live around Mount Kilimanjaro also speak Kichagga. With a friend, try practicing the Kichagga words below.

English	Kichagga
Hello	Jambo
Good bye	Kwaheri
No problem	Hakuna matata
Thank you	Asante
How are you?	Habari?
Very well	Mzuri sana

Kilimanjaro Timeline

Prehistoric

750,000 years ago Kilimanjaro's first volcano, Shira, forms.

500,000 years ago Mawenzi, its second volcano, forms.

460,000 years ago Kibo forms.

10,000 years ago Temperatures start to increase, and plants that need cold climates to survive retreat to mountain slopes.

1000 BC People live around the base of Mount Kilimanjaro.

Exploration

AD 1600s The Chagga move to the area.

1848 Johannes Rebmann becomes the first European to see Mount Kilimanjaro.

1861 Richard Thornton, of Great Britain, attempts to climb Mount Kilimanjaro. He does not reach the top.

1889 Germany's Dr. Hans Meyer and Austria's Ludwig Purtscheller become the first Europeans to reach the peak.

Development

Early 1900s Part of Mount Kilimanjaro is set aside as a game reserve.

1914 Frau von Ruckteschell becomes the first woman to climb Mount Kilimanjaro.

1921 The game reserve is made into a forest reserve as well.

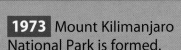

1973 Mount Kilimanjaro National Park is formed.

1977 The park opens to the public.

1989 Mount Kilimanjaro becomes a UNESCO World Heritage Site.

1993 The park creates a management plan that helps protect the mountain and minimize the effects of tourism.

Present

2001 Bruno Brunod of Italy becomes the fastest person to reach the summit. It takes him only 5 hours and 38 minutes.

2004 Tanzania's Simon Mtuy becomes the fastest person to summit and descend the mountain. He does this in 8 hours and 27 minutes.

2007 Scientists predict that Kilimanjaro will lose its icecap within 20 years due to climate change.

2012 American Spencer West, a double amputee, climbs Mount Kilimanjaro on his hands.

Protecting Kilimanjaro

A poor country such as Tanzania welcomes tourism. However, too many tourists can harm important sites, including Mount Kilimanjaro. Hiking trails cut through vegetation, and people who walk off the trails damage the plant life that lives on the mountain. Hikers can contribute to soil erosion simply by walking on the ground. When camps are set up for the night, some hikers cut down trees to use as firewood. Litter in the form of plastic bags, water bottles, toilet paper, and candy wrappers can be found on the ground.

In recent years, the park has been trying to stop these negative effects. Now, ecotourism practices are encouraged to keep the park free of clutter and preserve its natural appeal. Limits are placed on the number of people allowed into the park at one time. Trails are repaired when they become eroded, and people are no longer allowed to cut down trees. At one time, the remains of campfires and trash littered the mountain. Today, it is illegal to collect and burn plants on Kilimanjaro, and people must remove all items that they bring with them to the mountain.

Camping and other human activities can have detrimental effects on Kilimanjaro's natural environment.

Education programs have been developed to teach people about keeping Mount Kilimanjaro clean. Visitors, porters, wardens, guides, and people who live in the community are taught ways they can help preserve the mountain environment. They learn how to keep trails clean, report **poachers**, and spot forest fires.

Should visitors be allowed to climb Mount Kilimanjaro?	
Yes	**No**
Visitors bring money to a very poor country.	Visitors damage the plants and soil on the mountain.
People who see the mountain firsthand will want to help protect it.	People can experience the beauty of the mountain by simply viewing it.
Most visitors know how to properly dispose of their garbage.	Visitors litter the mountain with candy wrappers, plastic bags, and water bottles.

Natural Attractions

Each year, thousands of people attempt to hike to the summit of Mount Kilimanjaro. There are many routes up the mountain. Most people take four to six days to reach the top.

The hike can be done using standard hiking equipment. However, climbing Mount Kilimanjaro is still considered to be a huge challenge. Trying to climb the mountain too quickly is dangerous. This is because oxygen levels decrease as the altitude increases. There is half the amount of oxygen at the summit as there is at sea level. Climbers must let their bodies slowly adjust to the decreasing oxygen levels. If they do not, climbers may suffer from altitude sickness, an illness that causes headaches, sleepiness, and muscle weakness that can be deadly. In addition to a lack of oxygen, climbers must cover more than 50 miles (80 km) of land without the use of vehicles.

Mount Kilimanjaro is the setting for two athletic events. The Kilimanjaro Marathon is a 26.2-mile (42.2-km) foot race around the base of the mountain. Another event, the Kiliman Adventure Challenge, includes a climb to the summit, a mountain bike race, and a marathon.

To complete the Kiliman Adventure Challenge, participants must climb to the summit within six days, ride 118 miles (190 km) by bike, and run 26 miles (42.2 km). Competitors can enter the Challenge as individuals or as a team.

A National Park

Kilimanjaro's forests are home to a wide variety of plants, including 130 species of trees and 170 species of shrubs.

A large part of Mount Kilimanjaro is a national park. Mount Kilimanjaro National Park was formed in 1973, and it was opened to the public in 1977. It protects wildlife and maintains trails, and provides rescue teams for people who experience problems on the mountain.

The national park covers 292 square miles (755 sq km). It includes the areas above the tree line, as well as six **corridors** through the Kilimanjaro Forest Reserve. The reserve was created to keep the logging and farming industries from causing more damage to the rain forests.

In 1987, the mountain was named a United Nations Educational, Scientific and Cultural Organization (UNESCO) World Heritage Site. UNESCO identifies places around the world that are important to all people. These landmarks are protected from being destroyed by tourism and neglect.

Legends from Kilimanjaro

When Johannes Rebmann first saw Mount Kilimanjaro, the local people told him its summit was covered with a strange white powder that looked like silver. They believed that evil spirits protected the mountain's treasures, and they would punish any person who tried to climb the mountain. Rebmann soon learned that the silver was snow and that the evil spirits were the extreme cold. Both the snow and the cold could easily hurt a person who was not dressed for the weather.

The Chagga people still have great respect for the mountain. To them, it is the home of the gods. Traditionally, the Chagga would bury their dead so that the body was facing Mount Kilimanjaro. They may have believed that the summit led to the **afterlife**.

Kibo is the only one of Mount Kilimanjaro's three peaks that has permanent ice and snow.

Jagged Mawenzi

Mawenzi is known for its jagged peak. Scientists say that this peak formed as a result of erosion. The Chagga have a different story. They believe that the volcanoes were brothers who had a fight.

Mawenzi once looked like Kibo. One day, Mawenzi's fire died, so he asked Kibo for help. Kibo gave Mawenzi coal. Mawenzi decided this was a good way to get fire. Day after day, Mawenzi let his fire die. Each day, Kibo gave Mawenzi coal. However, Mawenzi never thanked Kibo for his generosity.

One day, Mawenzi saw that Kibo was not home. He decided to help himself to all of Kibo's coal. When Kibo returned and saw what Mawenzi had done, he was very mad. Kibo hit Mawenzi on the head, giving him the jagged peak he has today. Kibo had to work hard to restart his fire. This caused lava to spew from his belly.

At 16,893 feet (5,149 m) in height, Mawenzi is the second-highest summit of Mount Kilimanjaro.

True or False?

Decide whether the following statements are true or false. If the statement is false, make it true.

1. Mount Kilimanjaro is made up of three volcanoes.

2. Plants and animals are similar all over the mountain.

3. Some plants survive the cold by growing really big.

4. Uhuru Peak is Mount Kilimanjaro's highest point.

5. Most people in Tanzania speak Kichagga.

6. It is illegal to collect and burn plants on Mount Kilimanjaro.

ANSWERS
1. True. The volcanoes are Kibo, Mawenzi, and Shira.
2. False. There are many types of plants and animals.
3. True. Examples include lobelias and groundsels.
4. True. It is located on Kibo.
5. False. Kichagga is the language of the Chagga people, but most Tanzanians speak Swahili.
6. True.

Short Answer

Answer the following questions using information from the book.

1. What are two ways visitors can harm the mountain?

2. What is the Great Rift Valley?

3. What is magma called after it erupts?

4. Do monkeys live on Mount Kilimanjaro?

5. Who was the first European to see Mount Kilimanjaro?

Multiple Choice

Choose the best answer for the following questions.

1. What is the name of the people who live at the base of Mount Kilimanjaro?
   a. the Swahilians
   b. the Chagga
   c. the Kichagga

2. Which volcano has a jagged peak?
   a. Kibo
   b. Shira
   c. Mawenzi

3. Why is it dangerous to climb the mountain too fast?
   a. you may get tired
   b. your muscles might get sore
   c. you might get altitude sickness

4. What is an extinct volcano?
   a. a volcano that is no longer active
   b. a volcano that erupts once a year
   c. a volcano that could erupt at any time

Mountain Building

Earth's surface is made of a thin layer of rock called the crust. The crust is made of 12 tectonic plates. A river of hot magma flows under these plates, causing them to slowly shift toward and away from each other. Rocks are formed through the movement of tectonic plates. Try this exercise to see what happens to rocks when mountains form.

Materials

Foam sheets of different colors

String

Scissors

Instructions

1. With an adult's help, cut the foam into strips 2 to 4 inches (5 to 10 centimeters) wide and 8 to 12 inches (20 to 30 cm) long.

2. Cut two small holes into each end with the scissors.

3. Alternate thickness and color to create a stack of three to five pieces. These layers of foam represent layers of rock.

4. Thread the string through the holes cut in the foam to fasten the pieces together, forming a foam sandwich.

5. Make sure the string is loose enough that the foam pieces can slide when bent. By pushing and folding the foam, you can imagine how rock layers respond to the same forces.

Key Words

afterlife: life after death

altitude: the measurement above sea level of different locations on Earth

Christianity: a religion based on the teachings of Jesus Christ

corridors: long stretch of land between two areas

equator: the imaginary line that runs east to west around the widest part of Earth, dividing it in two

fault: a break in Earth's crust

heath: small leathery shrubs

ice ages: periods when Earth was covered with glaciers

insulation: the act of protecting something against heat loss

lava: hot, liquid rock that flows from a volcano

lichens: plant-like organisms that are able to grow in harsh conditions

missionary: a person who introduces a religion to people in other countries

plateau: an area of land having a raised, flat surface

poachers: people who hunt illegally

vegetation: the types of plants that are found in a specific area

Index

Log on to www.av2books.com

AV² by Weigl brings you media enhanced books that support active learning. Go to www.av2books.com, and enter the special code found on page 2 of this book. You will gain access to enriched and enhanced content that supplements and complements this book. Content includes video, audio, weblinks, quizzes, a slide show, and activities.

AV² Online Navigation

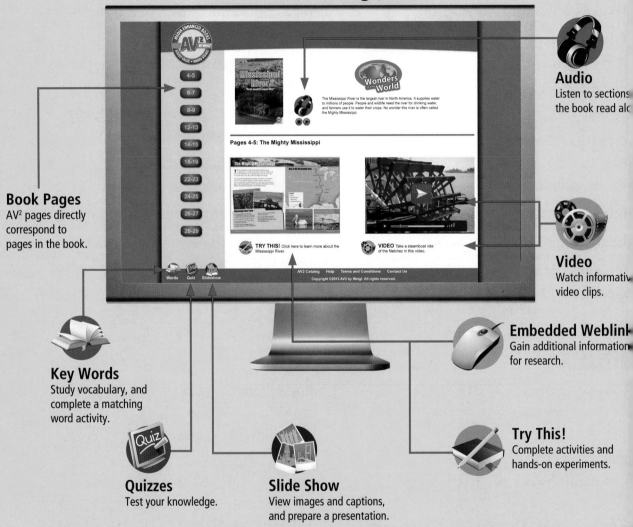

Book Pages
AV² pages directly correspond to pages in the book.

Audio
Listen to sections the book read al

Video
Watch informativ video clips.

Key Words
Study vocabulary, and complete a matching word activity.

Embedded Weblink
Gain additional information for research.

Quizzes
Test your knowledge.

Slide Show
View images and captions, and prepare a presentation.

Try This!
Complete activities and hands-on experiments.

AV² was built to bridge the gap between print and digital. We encourage you to tell us what you like and what you want to see in the future.

Sign up to be an AV² Ambassador at www.av2books.com/ambassador.